MANCHESTER CITY

THE OFFICIAL ANNUAL 2018

A Grange Publication

©2017 Published by Grange Communications Ltd., Edinburgh, under licence from Manchester City Football Club. Printed in the EU.

Written by David Clayton Designed by Simon Thorley
Photographs ©ManCity (thanks to Victoria Haydn)

ISBN: 978-1-911287-75-9

CONTENTS

AUGUST

City raced out of the blocks with a 100% record in August. A hard-fought 2-1 win over Sunderland was the perfect start to the season – even if the Blues had to rely on a late own goal to clinch the points. Then qualification to the Champions League group stage was all-but secured with a 5-0 first leg win away to Steaua Bucharest and then City thrashed Stoke City 4-1 at the Britannia Stadium. With 11 goals in the first three games and Sergio Aguero scoring six of them, the Blues were flying. A terrific month was completed with a 1-0 second leg win over Steaua and a 3-1 win over West Ham at the Etihad.

SEPTEMBER

After an international break, City returned to action with an impressive 2-1 win over Manchester United. Goals from Kevin De Bruyne and Kelechi Iheanacho secured three points at Old Trafford before the Champions League group stage kicked off a 4-0 win over Borussia Monchengladbach – Aguero scoring another hat-trick! City made it eight wins in a row with another big win – 4-0 over Bournemouth – to get to the top of the table. A much-changed side then beat Swansea City 2-1 in the EFL Cup before City beat the same side 3-1 in the league three days later. Ten wins in a row – Pep Guardiola could not have wished for a better start. The final game of the month brought the winning streak to an end in the Champions League as Celtic held City 3-3 in Glasgow.

October was the first indication that City may not have the title wrapped up by Christmas! Tottenham deservedly beat the Blues 2-0 at White Hart Lane and more points were dropped by the league leaders as Everton held City 1-1 at the Etihad. Though Barcelona beat the Blues 4-0 in the Champions League, the score didn't reflect how well City had played for the first 50 minutes or so. And the 1-1 draw at home to Southampton a few days later was not the reaction Guardiola was hoping for. City exited the EFL Cup with a 1-0 loss at Manchester United before returning to winning ways in the final match of October following a 4-0 triumph at West Brom.

DECEMBER

The race for the title swayed in Chelsea's favour when the teams met at the Etihad in early December. Leading 1-0, De Bruyne had a great chance to double the advantage but saw his close-range effort hit the bar. Moments later Chelsea levelled and went on to win 3-1. Another 1-1 home draw followed as Celtic ended the group stage of the Champions League, but a 4-2 loss to struggling champions Leicester left City further adrift of the leaders. Successive wins over Watford, Arsenal and Hull City put City back up to second, but a disappointing 1-0 loss to Liverpool was not the way the Blues wanted to end 2016.

NOVEMBER

November couldn't have started better as City produced a stunning performance to beat Barcelona 3-1 – the first win over the Catalans in six attempts. Goals from Kevin De Bruyne and Ilkay Gundogan (2) secured a famous win, but the Blues lost top spot in the Premier League when Middlesbrough scored a late equaliser to secure a 1-1 draw a few days later – City's third successive 1-1 draw in the league at the Etihad. Yaya Toure was finally recalled for the trip to Crystal Palace and repaid the manager with both goals in a 2-1 win. After drawing 1-1 with Monchengladbach, a hard-earned 2-1 win over Burnley at Turf Moor kept the Blues in touch with leaders Chelsea.

JANUARY

FEBRUARY

A narrow 2-1 win over Burnley started the New Year and a 5-0 FA Cup win over West Ham was arguably the best display of the season – but it was followed by the worst defeat of the campaign with Everton handing out a 4-0 thrashing at Goodison Park. City needed a lift against second placed Spurs in the next game and led 2-0, only to be pegged back 2-2 and see more points dropped at home. That saw City drop to fifth and with a fight to qualify for the 2017/18 Champions League. A 3-0 FA Cup win at Crystal Palace ended a mixed month for the Blues.

February proved to be a good month. Victories over West Ham, Swansea and Bournemouth put City back into second spot and the 0-0 draw with Huddersfield Town gave City a home replay and a chance to progress to the last 16. Then, the match of the season, City and Monaco produced a football feast of goals, the Blues edging a thrilling game at the Etihad 5-3.

MARCH

The goals kept coming with a comfortable 5-1 win over Huddersfield in the FA Cup followed by a 2-0 win at Sunderland. But the failure to beat another mid-table side at home meant Chelsea were now pulling clear at the top as this time Stoke left with a point following a 0-0 Etihad stalemate. A 2-0 win over Middlesbrough put the Blues into the FA Cup semi-final, but Monaco proved too strong in the return leg of the Champions League Round of 16 to progress 3-1 and win on away goals. The disappointment continued with yet another 1-1 draw at home, this time with Liverpool, meaning City had won just four of their last 11 home games.

APRIL
MAY

MAY

City's 2-2 draw away to Arsenal did little to help the Blues' hopes of finishing in the top four. A 2-1 defeat to Chelsea ended any lingering title hopes City fans might have had. Wins over Hull and Southampton saw the Blues go into the FA Cup semi with Arsenal at Wembley in good form. Despite taking a 60th minute lead through Aguero, the Gunners came back to win 2-1 in extra time, ending any hopes of a trophy in Pep's first season. Draws with Manchester United and Middlesbrough did little to lift the spirits with the Blues in a three-way battle for a top four finish.

As City have done so many times over the past few years, the Blues finished on a high. Crystal Palace were thrashed 5-0 before City recorded comfortable wins over Leicester and West Brom. The season finale was a stunning 5-0 win away to Watford, securing third spot in the table. There were lots of goals, entertaining football and the promise of plenty more to come!

GUESS WHO?#1

Here are four mystery City players – use your powers of observation and detective work to solve their identity – we didn't even need to disguise them...

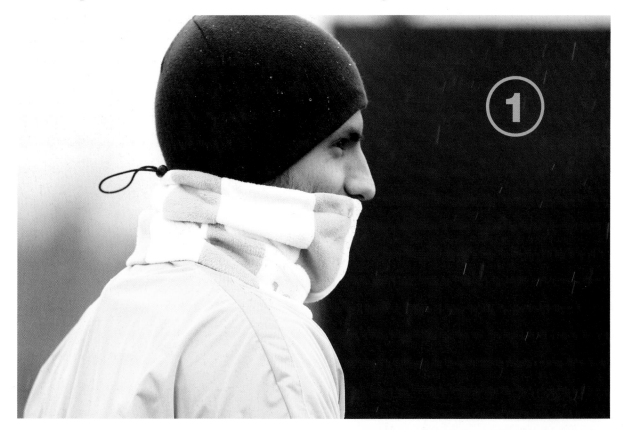

1) Recognise the eyes?
2) Somebody from warmer conditions perhaps?
3) Who is chatting with Pep Guardiola before training?
4) Heavily disguised but are there enough clues to figure out his identity?

Answers on page 60&61

MCFC PLAYER OF THE YEAR 2016/17:

DAVID SILVA

It was no surprise that David Silva was voted City's Player of the Year for 2016/17 – the only real shock is that this was the first time he's won the award!

To City fans, Silva is a genius – fantastic to watch as he glides around the pitch, effortlessly linking up play and creating opportunities for others.

Many wondered after the 2015/16 season whether David could reach the sort of highs he had in previous seasons ever again after probably his least magical season – after carrying an ankle injury for most of the season after a nasty challenge against Luxembourg side-lined him for several weeks.

Silva refused to rest, preferring to take painkilling injections, but it affected his performances. With new manager Pep Guardiola arriving, would Silva retain his place in the side?

Free from injury at last, he returned for the 2016/17 season and quickly showed he was not only back to his best, but he went on to have his best season yet for the Blues.

Silva was instrumental in everything good City did and he was named captain for many games in Vincent Kompany's absence.

Given a new role and extra freedom by Guardiola, the City fans' favourite excelled, playing more games, making more passes and performing better than ever.

He passed a number of career milestones for the Blues, making his 300th start, scoring his 50th goal and moving steadily up the list of Spain's all-time greats as he continued to be a vital part of the national team.

Now aged 31, it is incredible that this most gifted midfielder seems to be actually improving with age! With speed not a major part of his game, his vision and intelligence could continue to grace the City team for many more years.

Let's hope so – he is without doubt one of the greatest players to ever play for the club and many believe he is the best. Long may he reign!

FACTS AND STATS:

Appearances (all comps): 306

Goals: 51

During 2016/17, Silva played more minutes per game than any other season since he joined the Blues.

Since he arrived in 2010, his 64 assists is the highest of any player in the Premier League.

He is now Spain's fourth highest goal scorer of all time with 32 goals and has won 113 caps (to the end of the 2016/17 season).

In all competitions, his average of 81.02 minutes per game is more than three minutes more than his previous campaign and almost 10 minutes more than his first season in 2010/11.

Silva is a model of consistency, with his 86.72% passing accuracy virtually the same every season since he joined - it's slightly higher than last season and his highest since 2013/14.

With eight goals, he equalled his second highest tally for the Blues in 2016/17 and his 45 appearances were his most yet in one season for City.

He's nicknamed 'El Mago' which means 'The Magician' in Spanish. He is also known as 'Merlin' – another wizard!

THE BARNET FORMULA

The squad has got their hair styles all mixed-up, so, who's got who's?

NAME GAME

Can you figure out who the 11 City players are from the anagrams below...?

01. Nose Relay
02. Love Rind Is Ban
03. Great Elm Shiner
04. I Jab Less Gruel
05. My Pink Covenant
06. Derby Ink Venue
07. A Rye At You
08. Vivid Salad
09. Jots No Hens
10. Find An Heron
11. Unkind Yoga Gal

Answers on page 60&61

SPOT THE DIFFERENCE

There are 5 differences between Picture A and Picture B below – can you find them all?

Answers on page 60&61

SUMMER SIGNING #1
BERNARDO SILVA

Bernardo Silva became City's first signing of the season when he agreed to join the Blues back in June.

The Portuguese playmaker clearly impressed Pep Guardiola when City and Monaco met in the Champions League, after he helped the French side to the Ligue 1 title and the Champions League semi-finals.

Back story: Silva began his career at Benfica, where he impressed for their B side in the Segunda Division, and in the summer of 2013 he went to the Under 19 European Championships where he was named in the top 10 talents by UEFA reporters after helping Portugal to the semi-finals of the competition. He decided to move to Monaco in 2014, initially on loan, despite only playing three times for Benfica. He wasn't with his new club long before they decided to make it a permanent arrangement and in his first campaign he helped Monaco finish third in Ligue 1 as well as making the quarter-finals of the Champions League.

Having finished third in Ligue 1 again the following season, Leonardo Jardim's attacking revolution began to gather pace in 2016/17.

He had joined a talented side too, with players such as Radamel Falcao, Fabinho, Benjamin Mendy, Thomas Lemar and Kylian Mbappe.

The skilful Silva was a major influence in Monaco's stellar 2016/17 campaign as they went on to win the Ligue 1 title as well as beating Spurs, Borussia Dortmund and City during their epic Champions League adventure.

He made 51 appearances last season, scoring 10 goals and assisting a further 10 goals for his team-mates. Silva also made his senior international debut for Portugal in 2015 in a game against Cape Verde and already has 15 caps for his country.

NEED TO KNOW:

Name: Bernardo Mota Veiga de Carvalho e Silva
Age: 23
Born: Lisbon, Portugal (10 August 1994)
Height: 5 feet 8 inches
Position: Attacking midfielder
Squad number: 20
Previous clubs: Benfica, Monaco

HE SAYS:

"It feels great. To be honest I'm now at one of the best teams in the world. To be part of this club and to have this opportunity is great.

"I'm very happy to be part of Manchester City's team and I look forward to trying to do my best to help the team reach their goals."

"Of course when you have the opportunity of being trained by Pep Guardiola, you don't say no.

"As we all know, what he did in Barcelona and Bayern Munich was amazing and we expect also here that he will win titles. It's great to be working with him and to have this opportunity."

WHAT WE CAN EXPECT:

Bernardo has superb close control and plenty of tricks – he can dribble, beat players and work his way out of tight corners. He has fantastic vision and can create and score goals but loves nothing better than taking on two or three markers and then outsmarting them. Predominantly left-footed, City fans will love his box-of-tricks style and he should link up well with David Silva.

CROSSWORD

Can you solve the crossword below – it's all about last season and trust us it gets easier the more you answers you fill in!

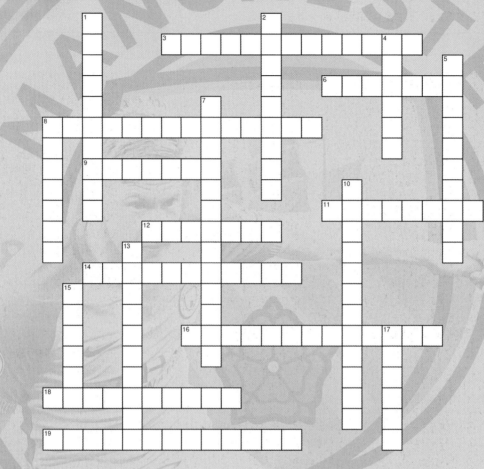

Across

3 Who did Yaya Toure score two goals against in his comeback game?

6 Which team were City playing when both Sergio Aguero and Fernandinho were sent off in 2016/17?

8 Who did Manchester City Women beat in Women's FA Cup final?

9 This team knocked City out of the FA Cup 11 Which Tottenham player scored against City at home and away in 2016/17?

12 Which club did Leroy Sane join City from?

14 Who did Brahim Diaz make his senior debut against?

16 Who is Manchester City Women' captain?

18 Who will be City's new No.5 this season?

19 Who scored the goal that knocked City out of the FA Cup last season?

Down

1 Who did City beat in Pep Guardiola's first game as City manager?

2 Which club did Gabriel Jesus join City from?

4 Patrick Roberts spent all least season on loan to which club?

5 Who was the MCFC Player of the Season?

7 Who left City after nine years at the end of the 2016/17 season?

8 Which club did Brazilian goalkeeper Ederson join City from?

10 Who was City's top scorer last season?

13 Who spent last season on loan with Sevilla?

15 From which team did Bernardo Silva sign?

17 Which club did Joe Hart spend last season on loan with?

Answers on page 60&61

SPOT THE BALL#1

Can you spot the ball? We've removed the real ball from the picture below so you'll have to use detective work to try and figure out exactly which grid it's in – it's tricky and maybe not as obvious as it first looks.

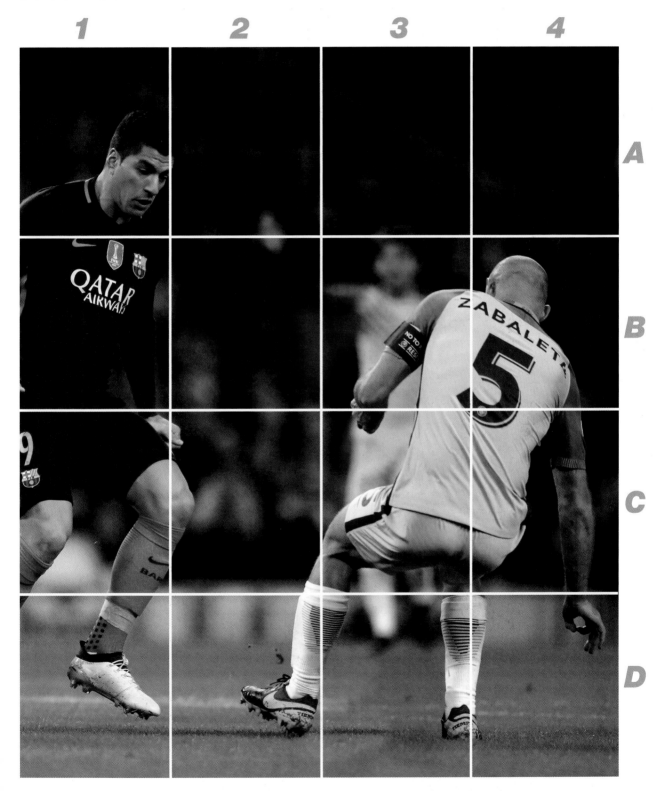

Answers on page 60&61

GOALSOF THESEASON2016/17

We've chosen 10 unforgettable goals from last year's campaign with our ratings out of five for importance and technique...

VINCENT KOMPANY
V CRYSTAL PALACE (May)

Importance: ☆☆
Technique: ☆☆☆☆☆

A goal made in Belgium! David Silva volleyed a high pass out to the right where Kevin De Bruyne was waiting – the City midfielder took his time as he weighed up his options and when he saw Vincent Kompany find space in the box, he crossed a low ball in and the skipper smashed the ball home from 12 yards out.

SERGIO AGUERO
V BURNLEY (January)

Importance: ☆☆☆
Technique: ☆☆☆☆

Raheem Sterling drove into the Burnley box before falling over keeper Tom Heaton and as the crowd appealed for a penalty, Sergio Aguero picked up the loose ball and hit a powerful angled shot that beat two defenders on the line.

YAYA TOURE
V CRYSTAL PALACE (November)

Importance: ☆☆☆☆
Technique: ☆☆☆☆

Having been out of the side for several months, Yaya Toure scored just before half-time as he waited for an opening, played a one-two with Nolito and then smashed a shot high into the roof of the net.

SERGIO AGUERO
V HULL CITY (April)

Importance: ☆☆☆
Technique: ☆

This was undoubtedly the worst finish of the season – but the build-up play was magnificent with every City player involved at some stage as the Blues knocked the ball around the pitch, finally ending with Sterling's dart past two defenders and his low cross was bundled home by Aguero.

ALEKS KOLAROV
V LEICESTER (December)

Importance: ☆
Technique: ☆☆☆☆

Aleks Kolarov scored a scorcher against Leicester a couple of years ago and he repeated the feat during the Blues' 4-2 loss at the King Power Stadium. A typical Kolarov free-kick, he curled the ball over the wall with pace and power and gave the keeper no chance.

SERGIO AGUERO
V WEST BROM
(October)

Importance: ☆☆☆
Technique: ☆☆☆☆

As City ran riot at the Hawthorns, the pick of the goals was another Aguero special as he dropped his shoulder, made a few yards' space and then cracked an unstoppable rising shot past Ben Foster and into the top corner.

KEVIN DE BRUYNE
V WEST BROM
(May)

Importance: ☆☆☆
Technique: ☆☆☆☆☆

De Bruyne was waiting on the edge of the box as the ball fell kindly to him and in an instant, he volleyed a vicious low shot that gave the goalkeeper no chance whatsoever. Fantastic technique by the Belgian.

YAYA TOURE
V CRYSTAL PALACE
(January)

Importance: ☆☆☆
Technique: ☆☆☆☆☆

How Yaya loves playing Crystal Palace! After scoring two against the Eagles a few months earlier he returned to Selhurst Park in the FA Cup to fire a superb free-kick over the wall and into the top corner.

KEVIN DE BRUYNE
V MAN UNITED
(September)

Importance: ☆☆☆☆
Technique: ☆☆☆

Chasing a long ball out for Aleks Kolarov, Kelechi Iheanacho flicked a header into the path of De Bruyne who then was clear on goal. As he approached David De Gea, he glanced at one corner of the goal and then fired the ball in the other with a pinpoint low shot.

RAHEEM STERLING
V WEST HAM
(August)

Importance: ☆☆☆☆
Technique: ☆☆☆☆☆

A lovely goal from the City winger. After Samir Nasri played a simple ball to David Silva, he then played Sterling in and he skipped past the keeper before rolling a cheeky shot past the keeper's outstretched arms and a defender from an almost impossible angle.

SPOT THE BALL #2

Can you spot the ball? We've removed the real ball from the picture below so you'll have to use detective work to try and figure out exactly which grid it's in – it's tricky and maybe not as obvious as it first looks.

Answers on page 60&61

GUESS WHO?#2

Here's another four disguised images – can you work out who the City players are just by the limited info available? Good luck!

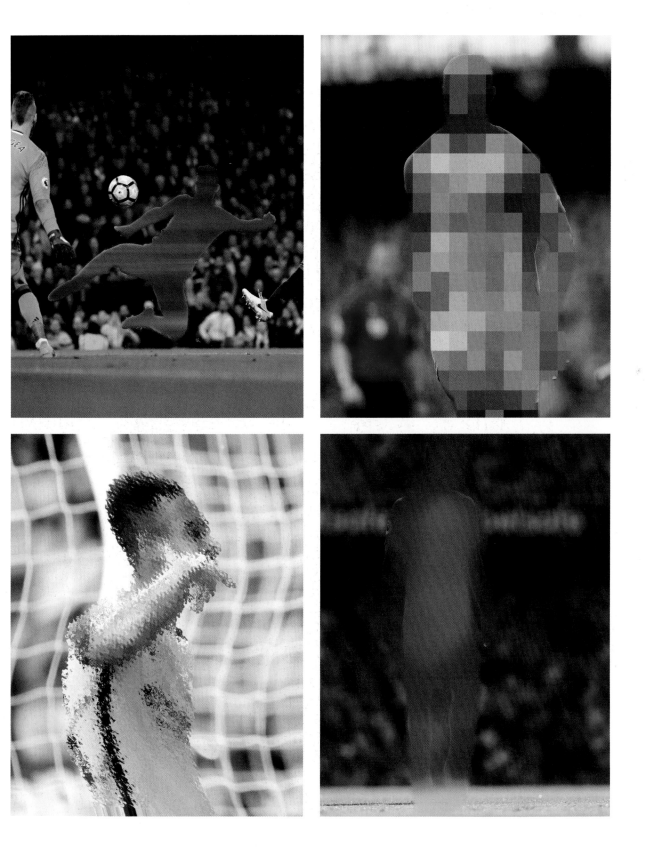

Answers on page 60&61

GABRIELJESUS

SUMMER SIGNING #3
KYLE WALKER

Kyle Walker joined City from Tottenham on a five-year deal in July 2017.

The England right-back opted to take the number two shirt previously worn by Bacary Sagna and became City's third signing of the 2017 close season.

Walker began his career at Sheffield United, where he spent a short period on loan at Northampton before returning to Bramhall Lane and impressing in the final few games of the 2008-09 season as the Blades made the Championship playoffs.

The 27-year-old signed for Tottenham that summer and was immediately loaned back to Sheffield United as part of the deal to ensure his progress continued.

But after impressing in the opening months of the 2009/10 season, he was recalled to Spurs and made two senior appearances.

Further loan moves followed, to QPR and Aston Villa, in a bid to secure further first-team experience but in 2011 he forced his way into the Spurs side and became their first-choice right-back.

In 2012, he was rewarded for a fine season by picking up the PFA Young Player of the Year award and has twice been named in the PFA Team of the Year.

He made 228 appearances for Tottenham in all competitions, scoring four goals, and last season helped them to second in the table, their highest league finish in the Premier League era.

His England debut came in the 1-0 win over Spain in 2011. He has 27 caps in total, with his most recent appearance coming as a second-half substitute in the 3-2 defeat to France at the Stade de France.

NEED TO KNOW:

Name: Kyle Andrew Walker
Born: 28/05/1990
Height: 6 foot
Position: Right-back
Squad number: 2
Previous clubs: Sheffield United, Northampton (loan), QPR (loan), Aston Villa (loan), Tottenham

HE SAYS:

"I am thrilled to be signing for City and can't wait to get started. Pep Guardiola is one of the most respected managers in the world and I feel he can help me take my game to a new level. This is the start of an exciting new chapter in my career and I couldn't be happier to be a City player."

WHAT WE CAN EXPECT:

Walker is regarded as one of the best – if not the best – attacking right-back in the Premier League.
A fearless, combative defender, Walker relishes being part of a side that loves to attack and he will be a valuable asset for the Blues in the coming seasons, with his speed and crossing accuracy part of the reason he established himself in the England team.

FUNNIES
Pictures taken last season that were just begging for a caption...

01

"Take a good look, Jesus. Is this the guy who ate your apple and hid your satsuma?"

02

Proof that Pep Guardiola really does have magical powers as he shrinks Ronald Koeman for pulling his tongue out.

03

Only a magician could make a ball levitate – so no surprises David Silva can!

04

"Wait guys! There's a wasp on the ball!"

05

"I know I'm suspended, Vinnie, but if I dress like this on the day the ref won't know who I am."

06

"Do I really have to write my own name and squad number on my shirt in felt-tip?"

07

"If you say I look daft, I'm going to bite you!"

08

"Order the pizza now and it'll be here on the final whistle!"

SUMMER SIGNING #4
BENJAMIN MENDY

Benjamin Mendy joined City from Monaco in July 2017.

The France international signed a five-year deal with the club and will wear the number 22 shirt.

Mendy began his career with Le Havre, where he played more than 50 league games, before joining Marseille in 2013.

He impressed at the Stade Velodrome, making 101 appearances in three seasons and establishing a reputation as one of the best full-backs in the French top flight.

Last summer, he joined Monaco on a five-year deal and his arrival saw a significant improvement in results for Leonardo Jardim's side.

Mendy's energy down the left was key to Monaco's attacking style as they won the Ligue 1 title and made it to the semi-finals of both the Champions League and the Coupe de France, scoring 159 goals in all competitions.

Their European run saw them take some notable scalps, beating Tottenham twice in the group stage, before knocking City and Borussia Dortmund out in the knock-out phase.

Mendy's performances were recognised in the end-of-season awards in France, with the left-back named in the Ligue 1 Team of the Year, and he was widely regarded as being one of the best attacking full-backs in the Champions League.

He made his senior international debut in March and looks set for a long international career. He is an exciting addition to Pep Guardiola's squad.

NEED TO KNOW:

Name: Benjamin Mendy
Born: 17/07/1994
Height: 6 feet 1 inches
Position: Left-back
Squad number: 22
Previous clubs: Le Havre, Le Havre II, Marseille, Monaco

HE SAYS:

"I am delighted to be joining Manchester City. They are one of Europe's leading clubs and in Pep Guardiola they have a manager committed to play attacking football. I am sure that over the next few years we will be successful.

"I am very excited – this is the move I wanted and after the French season was over, it was clear in my head that I wanted to join City. I will bring creativity and I can defend or provide assists for the strikers. I've always considered the Premier League to be the best in Europe and I'm looking forward to the next chapter of my career."

WHAT WE CAN EXPECT:

Calling Mendy just a defender would be like saying David Silva is just a midfielder!
Mendy is like an express down the left-flank, full of energy and a constant threat to the opposition.

He provides assists, is an excellent crosser but is also powerful and quick – City fans will likely soon make him a big crowd favourite!

WORDSEARCH #2

There are 20 words associated with matchday in the grid below - remember, the words could be horizontal, vertical or diagonal!

```
S  L  E  N  N  U  T  R  F  T  E  L  T  S  I  H  W
F  R  L  R  N  Y  B  N  U  L  P  V  C  N  R  L  P
M  B  E  E  J  Y  H  O  F  Y  A  O  H  P  G  L  H
M  F  T  T  B  Z  G  A  T  F  R  G  E  N  M  M  O
Z  N  T  S  R  U  J  V  L  E  O  M  S  U  W  X  T
R  R  Y  E  D  O  F  V  B  F  M  K  I  K  F  X  O
Y  L  H  H  L  G  P  O  K  A  T  D  C  K  Q  Q  G
Q  Z  H  C  H  D  A  P  R  N  A  I  M  I  N  M  R
V  B  K  N  K  R  H  G  U  T  L  O  M  R  K  K  A
J  H  V  O  D  Q  O  M  S  S  O  Y  B  E  T  J  P
W  S  C  O  V  R  X  D  D  N  X  R  N  F  C  T  H
N  E  F  M  P  M  A  H  B  V  M  F  M  E  L  V  E
S  V  P  R  W  H  T  E  B  H  A  B  Z  R  T  C  R
L  R  G  N  I  H  A  T  X  L  S  N  K  E  N  T  S
A  A  Z  T  N  M  M  X  L  M  C  C  Z  E  N  N  F
O  C  E  X  H  B  L  U  E  M  O  O  N  M  K  Y  G
G  S  H  O  T  D  O  G  T  X  T  J  M  M  C  X  Q
```

Moonchester	**Supporters**	**Whistle**
Etihad Stadium	**Scarves**	**Kick off**
Blue Moon	**Programme**	**Goals**
Half time	**Hot Dog**	**Dug out**
Referee	**Flags**	**Tunnel**
Scoreboard	**Mascot**	**Photographers**
Tunnel	**Moonbeam**	

Answers on page 60&61

LEROYSANE

SUMMER SIGNING#5
DANILO

Brazilian right-back Danilo joined City from Real Madrid in July 2017.

The 26-year-old signed a five-year deal and elected to take the No.3 shirt vacated by Bacary Sagna.

Danilo's senior career began at America Mineirão where he played a key role in their promotion from Serie C, before signing for Santos in 2010 where he spent two successful seasons.

Alongside Neymar and Alex Sandro, he was a revelation, and in 2011 he helped them win the Brazilian title and the Copa Libertadores, playing 37 matches in all competitions.

He played in both legs of the Copa Libertadores final - the first in central-midfield and the second at right-back - and scored the winning goal in the 2-1 win over Peñarol that saw them lift the most coveted trophy in South American football.

After playing in the 2012 FIFA Club World Cup, he moved to Europe, signing for Porto, and within two years had won back-to-back Primeira Liga titles, with his energy and industry from full-back making him one of the most sought-after players in the Portuguese top flight.

He soon began attracting the attention of Europe's biggest clubs, and in the summer of 2015 he moved to Real Madrid for 31.5 million, signing a six-year deal.

In total, he played 55 times for Los Blancos, winning one La Liga title, two Champions Leagues, a UEFA Super Cup and a FIFA Club World Cup.

With Kyle Walker and Benjamin Mendy also joining the Blues, Pep Guardiola will have an embarrassment of riches at his disposal for the 2017/18 season.

NEED TO KNOW:

Name: Danilo Luiz da Silva
Born: 15/07/1991
Height: 6 foot
Position: Right-back
Squad number: 3
Previous clubs: America MG, Santos, Porto, Real Madrid

HE SAYS:

"I am very, very happy to be joining Manchester City. There has been strong interest from other clubs, but it has always been my ambition to play for Pep Guardiola. As soon as I heard of his interest, I knew immediately I wanted to be a City player.

"I can't wait to get started and I'm looking forward to getting to know my new teammates over the coming weeks."

WHAT WE CAN EXPECT:

A typical Brazilian full-back, he is quick and attack-minded and can strike a ball with either foot, scoring several spectacular goals at club level. An attacking full-back in every sense of the word, Danilo can take penalties and has an impressive 25 goals in 257 career games at club level. He is comfortable at either end of the pitch and will share right-back duties with Kyle Walker.

WOMEN'S SUPER LEAGUE CHAMPIONS!

Manchester City Women have enjoyed a fantastic year, winning three major titles and reaching the semi-finals of the Champions League...

City finished FA Women's Super League champions for the first time, winning the title by five points. The Blues became the 'Indestructables', finishing unbeaten after 16 games and conceding just four goals all season. A fantastic achievement by Nick Cushing's side.

FA Cup Champions!

City landed their first FA Women's Cup in style, beating Birmingham City 4-1 in front of a record Wembley crowd of 35,271. Goals from Lucy Bronze, Izzy Christiansen, Carli Lloyd and Jill Scott ensured this team will go down in club history for yet another fantastic achievement!

Continental Cup Champions!

In what turned out to be the first trophy of the year, City beat Birmingham City 1-0 after extra time thanks to Lucy Bronze's winning goal. It is the second time City have won this trophy in three years.

Great Effort!

Manchester City Women's first adventure in the Champions League ended at the semi-final stage after an aggregate defeat to defending Champions League winners Olympic Lyonnaise. The damage was done in the first leg when the Blues were beaten 3-1 at the Academy Stadium but Carli Lloyd scored the only goal of the game as City won 1-0 in Lyon – a fantastic achievement – especially as Lyon went on to win the trophy again, beating PSG 7-6 on penalties in the final.

Captain Fantastic!

Proud City Women skipper Steph Houghton with the FA Cup, Women's Super League trophy and Continental Cup. An amazing year!

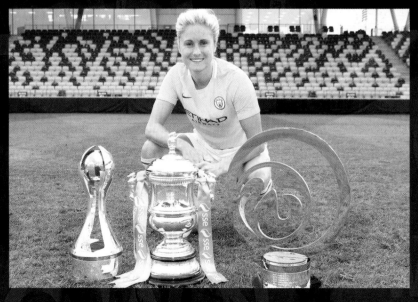

ONE2WATCH

PHIL FODEN

BRAHIM**DIAZ**

NAME: EDERSON MORAES
POSITION: GOALKEEPER
SQUAD NUMBER: 31

DATE OF BIRTH: 17/08/1993
PREVIOUS CLUBS: RIO AVE, BENFICA

2016/17 APPS (ALL COMPS): 0
2016/17 GOALS (ALL COMPS): 0
TOTAL CITY CAREER:
PLAYED: 0 GOALS: 0

NEW SIGNING!

EDERSON

NAME: CLAUDIO BRAVO
POSITION: GOALKEEPER
SQUAD NUMBER: 1

DATE OF BIRTH: 13/04/1983
PREVIOUS CLUBS: COLO COLO, REAL SOCIEDAD, BARCELONA

2016/17 APPS (ALL COMPS): 30
2016/17 GOALS (ALL COMPS): 0
TOTAL CITY CAREER:
PLAYED: 30 GOALS: 0

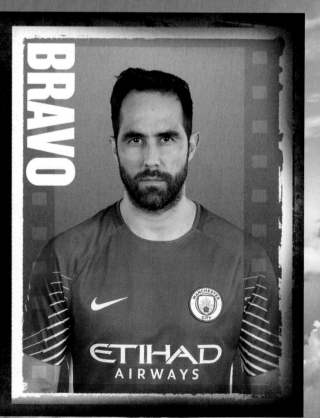

BRAVO

NAME: BENJAMIN MENDY
POSITION: LEFT-BACK
SQUAD NUMBER: 22

DATE OF BIRTH: 17/07/1994
PREVIOUS CLUBS: LE HARVE II, LE HARVE, MARSEILLE, MONACO

2016/17 APPS (ALL COMPS): 0
2016/17 GOALS (ALL COMPS): 0
TOTAL CITY CAREER: 0
PLAYED: 247 GOALS: 0

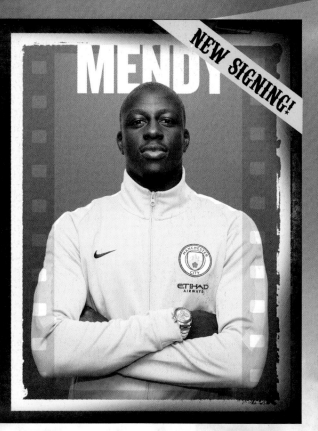

MENDY

NEW SIGNING!

NAME: VINCENT KOMPANY (CAPTAIN)
POSITION: CENTRAL DEFENDER
SQUAD NUMBER: 4

DATE OF BIRTH: 10/04/1986
PREVIOUS CLUBS: ANDERLECHT, SV HAMBURG

2016/17 APPS (ALL COMPS): 15
2016/17 GOALS (ALL COMPS): 3
TOTAL CITY CAREER:
PLAYED: 313 GOALS: 17

KOMPANY

NAME: TOSIN ADARABIOYO
POSITION: CENTRAL DEFENDER
SQUAD NUMBER: 53

DATE OF BIRTH: 24/09/1997
PREVIOUS CLUBS: ACADEMY
GRADUATE

2016/17 APPS (ALL COMPS): 3
2016/17 GOALS (ALL COMPS): 0
TOTAL CITY CAREER:
PLAYED: 4 GOALS: 0

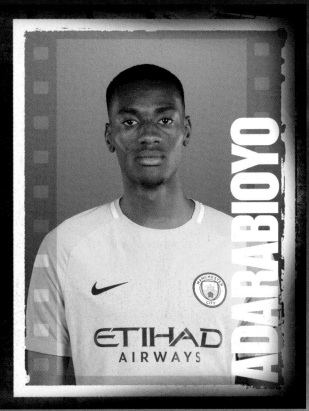

NAME: JOHN STONES
POSITION: CENTRAL DEFENDER
SQUAD NUMBER: 5

DATE OF BIRTH: 28/05/1994
PREVIOUS CLUBS: BARNSLEY, EVERTON

2016/17 APPS (ALL COMPS): 41
2016/17 GOALS (ALL COMPS): 2
TOTAL CITY CAREER:
PLAYED: 41 GOALS: 2

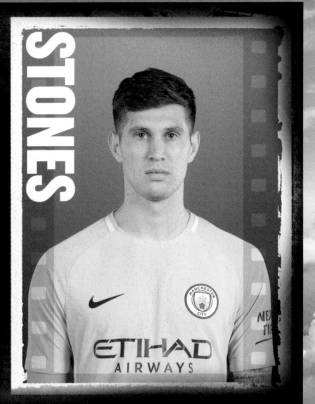

NAME: NICOLAS OTAMENDI
POSITION: CENTRAL DEFENDER
SQUAD NUMBER: 30

DATE OF BIRTH: 12/02/1988
PREVIOUS CLUBS: VELEZ SARSFIELD, PORTO, VALENCIA, ATLETICO MINEIRO (LOAN)
2016/17 APPS (ALL COMPS): 43
2016/17 GOALS (ALL COMPS): 1
TOTAL CITY CAREER:
PLAYED: 92 GOALS: 2

NAME: KYLE WALKER
POSITION: RIGHT-BACK
SQUAD NUMBER: 2

DATE OF BIRTH: 28/05/1990
PREVIOUS CLUBS: SHEFFIELD UNITED, NORTHAMPTON TOWN (LOAN) TOTTENHAM, LEICESTER (LOAN), QPR (LOAN), ASTON VILLA (LOAN)

2016/17 APPS (ALL COMPS): 0
2016/17 GOALS (ALL COMPS): 0
TOTAL CITY CAREER:
PLAYED: 0 GOALS: 0

NEW SIGNING!

NAME: DAVID SILVA
POSITION: ATTACKING MIDFIELD
SQUAD NUMBER: 21

DATE OF BIRTH: 08/01/1986
PREVIOUS CLUBS: VALENCIA, EIBAR
(LOAN), CELTA VIGO (LOAN)

2016/17 APPS (ALL COMPS): 45
2016/17 GOALS (ALL COMPS): 8
TOTAL CITY CAREER:
PLAYED: 306 GOALS: 51

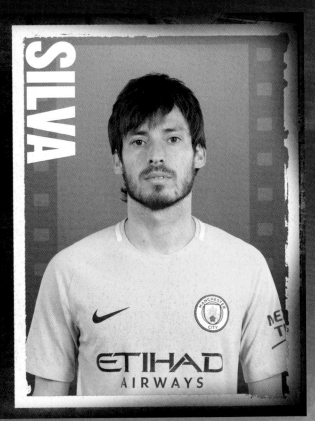

NAME: SERGIO AGUERO
POSITION: STRIKER
SQUAD NUMBER: 10

DATE OF BIRTH: 02/06/1988
PREVIOUS CLUBS: INDEPENDIENTE,
ATLETICO MADRID

2015/16 APPS (ALL COMPS): 45
2015/16 GOALS (ALL COMPS): 33
TOTAL CITY CAREER:
PLAYED: 262 GOALS: 169

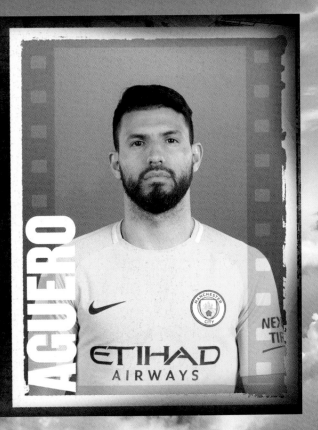

NAME: RAHEEM STERLING
POSITION: MIDFIELD
SQUAD NUMBER: 7

DATE OF BIRTH: 08/12/1994
PREVIOUS CLUBS: LIVERPOOL

2015/16 APPS (ALL COMPS): 47
2015/16 GOALS (ALL COMPS): 10
TOTAL CITY CAREER:
PLAYED: 94 GOALS: 21

NAME: GABRIEL JESUS
POSITION: STRIKER
SQUAD NUMBER: 33

DATE OF BIRTH: 03/04/1997
PREVIOUS CLUBS: PALMEIRAS

2015/16 APPS (ALL COMPS): 11
2015/16 GOALS (ALL COMPS): 7
TOTAL CITY CAREER:
PLAYED: 11 GOALS: 7

PHIL**FODEN**

Quiz&Puzzle Answers

GUESS WHO? #1
(From page 10&11)

SERGIO AGUERO ①

GABRIEL JESUS ②

DAVID SILVA ③

ILKAY GUNDOGAN ④

SPOT THE DIFFERENCE
(From page 15)

ORANGE TRIANGLE

GREEN JERSEY

EARPHONES ON CAMERMAN

YAYA NAME

STERLING NAME

HAIR SWAP
(From page 14)

KOMPANY'S HEAD, SANE'S HAIR

STERLING'S HEAD, JESUS' HAIR

AGUERO'S HEAD, OTAMENDI'S HAIR

TOURE'S HEAD, DE BRUYNE'S HAIR

CROSSWORD (From page 18)

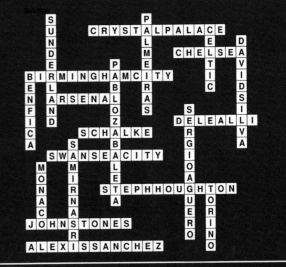

SPOT THE BALL #1
(From page 19)

NAME GAME
(From page 14)

01. NOSE RELAY (LEROY SANE)
02. LOVE RIND IS BAN (BERNARDO SILVA)
03. GREAT ELM SHINER (RAHEEM STERLING)
04. I JAB LESS GRUEL (GABRIEL JESUS)
05. MY PINK COVENANT (VINCENT KOMPANY)
06. DERBY INK VENUE (KEVIN DE BRUYNE)
07. A RYE AT YOU (YAYA TOURE)
08. VIVID SALAD (DAVID SILVA)
09. JOTS NO HENS (JOHN STONES)
10. FIND AN HERON (FERNANDINHO)
11. UNKIND YOGA GAL (ILKAY GUNDOGAN)

```
V I N C E N T K O M P A N Y N V V
R W G R G V Z H G Y N R T I N S N
F A I C R A G X I E L A C Z O E Z
N P H D S Q M R X P G O D B S R H
A E L E M U R V B L Y A J R G E B
R R T A T M Q E S V L R W C D N T
V L B Y S K S O J I P E X Z E A Q
S L T J B Y T T S L R F K M W G N
D K K N N A O O E U E F R Z R U M
I C K K M K D R O R X I L K T E R
V X E L R B T E J L J R F L R
A K N V A P A Y K L B I L B K O
D D K N Y Y P W X T F K N G A K V
I L R K A H V H Y D G R Z G T G Z
W E D Y P H J O H N S T O N E S R
B D T K E V I N D E B R U Y N E M
```

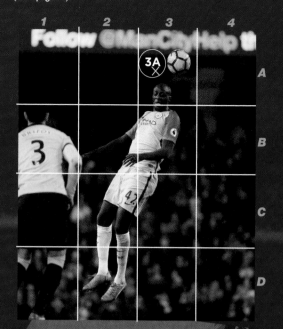

THE BIG CITY QUIZ 2018
(From page 26&27)

01. FALSE
02. KELECHI IHEANACHO
03. 33
04. WEST HAM
05. TRUE
06. TOTTENHAM
07. BOURNEMOUTH
08. DAVID SILVA
09. CELTIC
10. OLEXANDR ZINCHENKO
11. MANCHESTER UNITED
12. PATRICK ROBERTS
13. AARON MOOY
14. CARLI LLOYD
15. CHELSEA
16. ILKAY GUNDOGAN
17. BERNARDO SILVA
18. EVERTON 4-0
19. TRUE
20. BURNLEY
21. RED BULL SALZBURG
22. WEST HAM
23. FALSE - IT WAS CHELSEA
24. VINCENT KOMPANY
25. ARSENAL
26. 10
27. NO.23
28. KEZ BROWN
29. MIKEL ARTETA
30. ONCE
31. WATFORD
32. STEAUA BUCHAREST
33. HAMBURG
34. EDIN DZEKO
35. DE BRUYNE & IHEANACHO
36. RANGERS
37. DAVID SILVA
38. TRUE
39. CITY OF MANCHESTER STADIUM
40. MIDDLESBROUGH

SERGIO AGUERO

VINCENT KOMPANY

GABRIEL JESUS

JOHN STONES

```
S L E N N U T R F T E L T S I H W
F R L R N Y B N U L P V C N R L P
M B E E J Y H O F Y A O H P G L L
M F T T B Z G T F R G E N M M O
Z N T S R U J V L E O M S U W X T
R R Y E D O F V B F M K F X O
Y L H H L G P O K A T D C K Q Q G
Q Z H C H D A P R N A I M I N M R
V B K N K R H G U T L R K A P
J H V O D Q O M S S O Y B E T J H
W S C O V R X D D N X R N F C T P
N E F M P M A H B V M F M E L V E
S V P R W H T E B H A B Z R T C S
L R G N I H A T X L S N K E N S
A Z T N M M X L M C C Z E N N F
O C E X H B L U E M O O N M K Y G
G S H O T D O G T X T J M M C X Q
```

WHERE IS
GABRIEL JESUS?